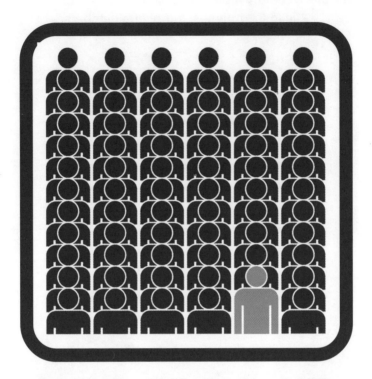

BEING SINGLE AND
THE SPIRITUAL QUEST

GROUP DIRECTORY

Pass this Directory around and have your Group Members
fill in their names and phone numbers

Name

Phone

_____   _____

_____   _____

_____   _____

_____   _____

_____   _____

_____   _____

_____   _____

_____   _____

_____   _____

_____   _____

_____   _____

_____   _____

_____   _____

_____   _____

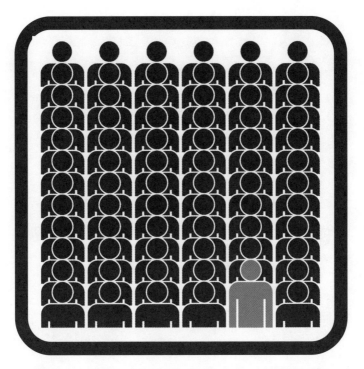

BEING SINGLE AND THE SPIRITUAL QUEST

EDITING AND PRODUCTION TEAM:
Keith Madsen, James F. Couch, Jr., Greg Benoit,
Katharine Harris, Scott Lee

SERENDIPITY
HOUSE

NASHVILLE, TENNESSEE

Published by Serendipity House Publishers
Nashville, Tennessee

International Standard Book Number: 1-57494-110-0

ACKNOWLEDGMENTS

Scripture quotations are taken from the Holman Christian Standard Bible unless
otherwise noted, © Copyright 2000 by Holman Bible Publishers.
Used by permission.

To Zondervan Bible Publishers
for permission to use the NIV text,
The Holy Bible, New International Bible Society.
© 1973, 1978, 1984 by International Bible Society.
Used by permission of Zondervan Bible Publishers.

Nashville, Tennessee
1-800-525-9563
www.serendipityhouse.com

TABLE OF CONTENTS

CORE VALUES

Community: The purpose of this curriculum is to build community within the body of believers around Jesus Christ.

Group Process: To build community, the curriculum must be designed to take a group through a step-by-step process of sharing your story with one another.

Interactive Bible Study: To share your "story," the approach to Scripture in the curriculum needs to be open-ended and right brain—to "level the playing field" and encourage everyone to share.

Developmental Stages: To provide a healthy program throughout the four stages of the life cycle of a group, the curriculum needs to offer courses on three levels of commitment: (1) Beginner Level—low-level entry, high structure, to level the playing field; (2) Growth Level—deeper Bible study, flexible structure, to encourage group accountability; (3) Discipleship Level—in-depth Bible study, open structure, to move the group into high gear.

Target Audiences: To build community throughout the culture of the church, the curriculum needs to be flexible, adaptable and transferable into the structure of the average church.

Mission: To expand the Kingdom of God one person at a time by filling the "empty chair." (We add an extra chair to each group session to remind us of our mission.)

INTRODUCTION

Each healthy small group will move through various stages as it matures.

STAGE ONE

Birth Stage: This is the time in which group members form relationships and begin to develop community. The group will spend more time in ice-breaker exercises, relational Bible study and covenant building.

STAGE TWO

Growth Stage: Here the group begins to care for one another as it learns to apply what they learn through Bible study, worship, and prayer.

STAGE FOUR

Multiply Stage: The group begins the multiplication process. Members pray about their involvement in new groups. The "new" groups begin the life cycle again with the Birth Stage.

STAGE THREE

Develop Stage: The inductive Bible study deepens while the group members discover and develop gifts and skills. The group explores ways to invite their neighbors and coworkers to group meetings.

Subgrouping: If you have nine or more people at a meeting, Serendipity recommends you divide into subgroups of 3–6 for the Bible study. Ask one person to be the leader of each subgroup and to follow the directions for the Bible study. After 30 minutes, the Group Leader will call "time" and ask all subgroups to come together for the Caring Time.

Each group meeting should include all parts of the "three-part agenda."

 Icebreaker: Fun, history-giving questions are designed to warm the group and to build understanding about the other group members. You can choose to use all of the Icebreaker questions, especially if there is a new group member that will need help in feeling comfortable with the group.

One of the purposes of this book is to begin a group. Therefore, getting to know one another and bonding together are essential to the success of this course. The goal is to get acquainted during the Icebreaker part of each group session.

 Bible Study: The heart of each meeting is the reading and examination of the Bible. The questions are open, discover questions that lead to further inquiry. Reference notes are provided to give everyone a "level playing field." The emphasis is on understanding what the Bible says and applying the truth to real life. The questions for each session build. There is always at least one "going deeper" question provided. You should always leave time for the last of the "questions for interaction." Should you choose, you can use the optional "going deeper" question to satisfy the desire for the challenging questions in groups that have been together for a while.

To help bond together as a group, it is important for everyone to participate in the Bible Study. There are no right or wrong answers to the questions. The group members should strive to make all of the other group members feel comfortable during the Bible Study time. Because we all have differing levels of biblical knowledge, it is essential that we appreciate the personal context from which answers are given. We don't have to know much about Scripture to bring our own perspectives on the truths contained in the Scriptures. It is vital to keep encouraging all group members to share what they are observing as we work through these important Bible passages.

 Caring Time: All study should point us to actions. Each session ends with prayer and direction in caring for the needs of the group members. You can choose between several questions. You should always pray for the "empty chair." Who do you know that could fill that void in your group?

Small groups help the larger body of Christ in many ways: caring for individuals, holding one another up in prayer, providing emotional support and in bringing new people into the body through filling the empty chair. Each week it is important to remember to pray for those who God would bring to fill your empty chair.

SHARING YOUR STORY: These sessions are designed for members to share a little of their personal lives each time. Through a number of special techniques, each member is encouraged to move from low risk, less personal sharing to higher risk responses. This helps develop the sense of community and facilitates caregiving.

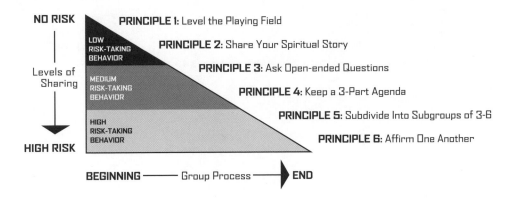

GROUP COVENANT: A group covenant is a "contract" that spells out your expectations and the ground rules for your group. It's very important that your group discuss these goals—preferably as part of the first session.

GROUND RULES:

- **Priority:** While you are in the group, you give the group meeting priority.

- **Participation:** Everyone participates and no one dominates.

- **Respect:** Everyone is given the right to their own opinion and all questions are encouraged and respected.

- **Confidentiality:** Anything that is said in the meeting is never repeated outside the meeting.

- **Empty Chair:** The group stays open to new people at every meeting.

- **Support:** Permission is given to call upon each other in time of need—even in the middle of the night.

- **Advice Giving:** Unsolicited advice is not allowed.

- **Mission:** We agree to do everything in our power to start a new group as our mission.

GOALS:

- The time and place this group is going to meet is _____.

- Responsibility for refreshments is _____.

- Child care is _____ responsibility.

- This group will meet until _____ at which time we will decide to split into new groups or continue our sessions together.

- Our primary purpose for meeting is: _____.

OUR SMALL GROUP COVENANT

1. The facilitator for this group is _____.

2. The apprentice facilitator for this group is _____.

3. This group will meet from _____ to _____ on _____.

4. This group will normally meet at _____.

5. Child care will be arranged by _____.

6. Refreshments will be coordinated by _____.

7. Our primary purpose for meeting is _____.

8. Our secondary purpose for meeting is _____.

9. We all agree to follow the ground rules listed below:

    a. This meeting will be given priority in our schedules.

    b. Everyone will participate in each meeting and no one will dominate a meeting.

    c. Each has a right to one's own opinion and all questions will be respected.

    d. Everything that is said in group meetings is never to be repeated outside of the meeting.

    e. This group will be open to new people at every meeting.

    f. Permission is given for all to call on each other in time of need.

    g. Unsolicited advice is not allowed.

    h. We agree to fill the empty chair and work toward starting new groups.

10. We are to hold one another accountable to meet any commitments mutually agreed upon by this group.

I agree to all of the above _____ date _____

FELT NEED SURVEY

Rank the following factors in order of importance to you with 1 being the highest and 5 being the lowest:

_____ The passage of Scripture that is being studied.

_____ The topic or issue that is being discussed.

_____ The affinity of group members (age, vocation, interest).

_____ The mission of the group (service projects, evangelism, starting groups).

_____ Personal encouragement.

Rank the following spiritual development needs in order of interest to you with 1 being the highest and 5 being the lowest:

_____ Learning how to become a follower of Christ.

_____ Gaining a basic understanding of the truths of the faith.

_____ Improving my disciplines of devotion, prayer, reading Scripture.

_____ Gaining a better knowledge of what is in the Bible.

_____ Applying the truths of Scripture to my life.

Of the various studies below, check the appropriate boxes that indicate: if you would be interested in studying for your personal needs (P), you think would be helpful for your group (G), or you have friends that are not in the group that would come to a study of this subject (F).

	P	G	F
Growing in Christ Series (7-week studies)			
Keeping Your Cool: Dealing with Stress	○	○	○
Personal Audit: Assessing Your Life	○	○	○
Seasons of Growth: Stages of Marriage	○	○	○
Checking Your Moral Compass: Personal Morals	○	○	○
Women of Faith (8 weeks)	○	○	○
Men of Faith	○	○	○
Being Single and the Spiritual Quest	○	○	○
Becoming a Disciple (7-week studies)			
Discovering God's Will	○	○	○
Time for a Checkup	○	○	○
Learning to Love	○	○	○
Making Great Kids	○	○	○
Becoming Small Group Leaders	○	○	○
Foundations of the Faith (7-week studies)			
Knowing Jesus	○	○	○
Foundational Truths	○	○	○
The Christian in a Postmodern World	○	○	○
God and the Journey to Truth	○	○	○

	P	G	F

Understanding the Savior (13-week studies)

	P	G	F
Mark 1–8: Jesus, the Early Years	○	○	○
Mark 8–16: Jesus, the Final Days	○	○	○
John 1–11: God in the Flesh	○	○	○
John 12–21: The Passion of the Son	○	○	○
The Miracles of Jesus	○	○	○
The Life of Christ	○	○	○
The Parables of Jesus	○	○	○
The Sermon on the Mount: Jesus, the Teacher	○	○	○

The Message of Paul

	P	G	F
Romans 1–7: Who We Really Are (13 weeks)	○	○	○
Romans 8–16: Being a Part of God's Plan (13 weeks)	○	○	○
1 Corinthians: Taking on Tough Issues (13 weeks)	○	○	○
Galatians: Living by Grace (13 weeks)	○	○	○
Ephesians: Together in Christ (12 weeks)	○	○	○
Philippians: Running the Race (7 weeks)	○	○	○

Words of Faith

	P	G	F
Acts 1–14: The Church on Fire (13 weeks)	○	○	○
Acts 15–28: The Irrepressible Witness (13 weeks)	○	○	○
Hebrews: Jesus the True Messiah (13 weeks)	○	○	○
James: Faith at Work (12 weeks)	○	○	○
Peter: Staying the Course (10 weeks)	○	○	○
1 John: Walking in the Light (11 weeks)	○	○	○
Revelation 1–12: End of Time (13 weeks)	○	○	○
Revelation 13–22: The New Jerusalem (13 weeks)	○	○	○

301 Bible Studies with Homework Assignments (13-week studies)

	P	G	F
Ephesians: Our Riches in Christ	○	○	○
James: Walking the Talk	○	○	○
Life of Christ: Behold the Man	○	○	○
Miracles: Signs and Wonders	○	○	○
Parables: Virtual Reality	○	○	○
Philippians: Joy Under Stress	○	○	○
Sermon on the Mount: Examining Your Life	○	○	○
1 John: The Test of Faith	○	○	○

Felt Need Series (7-week studies)

	P	G	F
Stress Management: Finding the Balance	○	○	○
12 Steps: The Path to Wholeness	○	○	○
Divorce Recovery: Picking Up the Pieces	○	○	○
Parenting Adolescents: Easing the Way to Adulthood	○	○	○
Blended Families: Yours, Mine, Ours	○	○	○
Dealing with Grief and Loss: Hope in the Midst of Pain	○	○	○
Healthy Relationships: Living Within Defined Boundaries	○	○	○
Marriage Enrichment: Making A Good Marriage Better	○	○	○

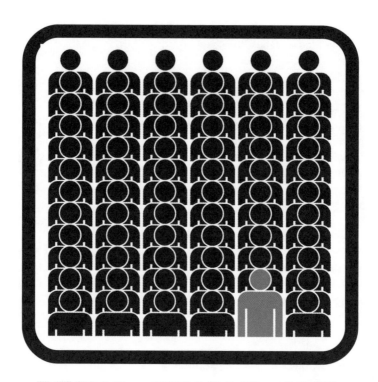

BEING SINGLE AND
THE SPIRITUAL QUEST

Session 1

HAGAR: SEEING GOD'S PROVISION

Scripture **Genesis 21:1–21**

 Welcome to this study for single adults on our spiritual quest. Together we will consider the stories of seven single adults in Scripture and what their stories can mean for our own spiritual journeys. We will discover that being single in this world does not make us alone, and that we are part of a family of faith that can bring to us love and fulfillment.

Much more so than in modern times, people in Bible times lived in a world built around couples and two-parent (or even multi-parent) families. However, even in this context we read in the Bible of single adults who played prominent roles in the story of God's people, and who even today can serve as examples to us. By looking at the lives of these single adults we can learn how God has worked to love, support, and use single adults, and we can relate our own lives to theirs. In this study we will look at the following stories of biblical singles and what they have to say to us:

• Hagar: a slave woman who neither had a choice in becoming Abraham's concubine nor in being divorced by him. She learned that God provides in the most dire circumstances.
• Ruth: a young widow who became an example of loyalty when she stuck by her widowed mother-in-law. By sticking together and supporting each other, these widows were able to make it through to better times.
• Mary and Martha: These single sisters who lived with their brother had contrasting personalities. Looking at their differences will help us discover what it means to set the right priorities in life.
• Mary Magdalene: One of Jesus' most loyal and devoted followers, this woman has much to teach us about faithfulness and a servant lifestyle.
• Paul: The most important evangelist in Christian history, this apostle was an advocate for the single lifestyle. He wrote and modeled how singles can have an advantage over married persons in showing single-minded devotion to our Lord.
• Lydia: A wealthy business woman who opened her heart and her home to help the gospel thrive in Europe.
• Jesus: We sometimes forget that our Lord himself was a single adult! But who did he say was his true family? By examining this story, we can get a new understanding of what "family" means and what it means to be truly alone.

In looking at these singles of biblical times, we need to remember that two realities generally held true: (1) Single women in Israel were generally poor. Women most often did not inherit property, and there were very few jobs available to them. Widows had to rely on the financial support of the community (see Acts 6:1–7), while divorced women were often outcasts (see John 4: 1–42). (2) Being a single man was also sometimes looked down upon, especially if one had never married.

Regardless of the societal feeling about these singles, the most important fact is that God valued and used them for his glory. The same is true for those of us who are single today.

Icebreaker : 15 min.
CONNECT WITH YOUR GROUP

Leader

Be sure to read the introductory material in the front of this book prior to the first session. To help your group members get acquainted, have each person introduce him or herself and then take turns answering one or two of the Icebreaker questions. If time allows, you may want to discuss all three questions.

One thing children often enjoy is parties where they are the center of attention. What do you remember most about the parties of your childhood? Share something about yourself by answering the following questions.

1. Finish this sentence: "The best party I remember having as a child was when...."

2. If you could have planned any kind of party you wanted when you were in grade school, which of the following would you have most wanted to happen at your party?
   ○ Pony rides.
   ○ A clown.
   ○ Lots of cake and ice cream.
   ○ Cool games like at an arcade or laser tag center.
   ○ Other _____.

3. What people would have to be there for your party to be all that you wanted?
   ○ My best friend, _____.
   ○ Both of my parents.
   ○ My favorite entertainer or sports figure.
   ○ A favorite relative.
   ○ Other _____.

Bible Study : 30 min.
READ SCRIPTURE + DISCUSS

Leader
Select two members of the group ahead of time to read aloud the Scripture passage. Then discuss the Questions for Interaction, dividing into subgroups of three to six. Be sure to save time at the end for the Caring Time.

In an economy built around two-income families, singles may find their financial resources coming up a little short. When that happens, where is God, and what kind of help can we expect from him? In this story we find a woman who had to struggle with these issues. As we consider how God related to her, we will be able to see more clearly how God can provide for the struggling single today. Read Genesis 21:1–21, and then use the questions that follow to explore the passage with your group. Be sure to save time at the end for the Caring Time.

Reader One: **21** Now the Lord was gracious to Sarah as he had said, and the Lord did for Sarah as he had promised. ²Sarah became pregnant and bore a son to Abraham in his old age, at the very time that God had promised him. ³Abraham gave the name Isaac to the son Sarah bore him. ⁴When his son Isaac was eight days old, Abraham circumcised him, as God commanded him. ⁵Abraham was a hundred years old when his son Isaac was born to him.

Reader Two: ⁶Sarah said, "God has brought me laughter, and everyone who hears about this will laugh with me." ⁷And she added, "who would have said to Abraham that Sarah would nurse children? Yet I have borne him a son in his old age."

Reader One: ⁸The child grew and was weaned, and on the day Isaac was weaned Abraham held a great feast. ⁹But Sarah saw the son whom Hagar the Egyptian had borne to Abraham was mocking, ¹⁰and she said to Abraham,

Reader Two: "Get rid of that slave woman and her son, for that slave woman's son will never share in the inheritance with my son Isaac."

Reader One: ¹¹The matter distressed Abraham greatly because it concerned his son. ¹²But God said to him, "Do not be so distressed about the boy and your maidservant. Listen to whatever Sarah tells you, because it is through Isaac that your offspring will be reckoned. ¹³I will make the son of the maidservant into a nation also, because he is your offspring."

¹⁴Early the next morning Abraham took some food and a skin of water and gave them to Hagar. He set them on her shoulders and then sent her off with the boy.

Reader Two: She went on her way and wandered in the desert of Beersheba. ¹⁵When the water in the skin was gone, she put the boy under one of the bushes. ¹⁶Then she went off and sat down nearby, about a bow-shot away, for she thought, "I cannot watch the boy die." And as she sat there nearby, she began to sob.

Reader One: ¹⁷God heard the boy crying, and the angel of God called to Hagar from heaven and said to her, "What is the matter, Hagar? Do not be afraid: God has heard the boy crying as he lies there. ¹⁸Lift the boy up and take him by the hand, for I will make him into a great nation."

¹⁹Then God opened her eyes and she saw a well of water. So she went and filled the skin with water and gave the boy a drink. ²⁰God was with the boy as he grew up. He lived in the desert and became an archer. ²¹While he was living in the desert of Paran, his mother got a wife for him from Egypt.

Genesis 21:1–21 (NIV)

 # QUESTIONS FOR INTERACTION

Leader

Refer to the Summary and Study Notes at the end of this section as needed. If 30 minutes is not enough time to answer all of the questions in this section, conclude the Bible Study by answering questions 6 and 7.

1. In what way are you most like Hagar?

2. Sarah was the one who wanted Abraham to take Hagar and have a child with her in the first place (see notes). Given that as background, how do you think Hagar must have felt about being left on her own with a son?

○ Angry and spiteful.
○ Frightened and uncertain of the future.
○ Confident that God would provide for her and her son.
○ Other _____.

3. What do you think Hagar was feeling when...
   ○ Sarah had a son?
   ○ Abraham sent her away?
   ○ She ran out of provisions?

4. What does Abraham give Hagar to take care of the boy? Why so little? How would that scanty provision have affected her?

5. When God answers Hagar and her son, what does he do to help her? Have you seen God's provision for your own situation?

6. When have you felt like Hagar when she placed her son under the bush—out of resources and out of hope?

7. When has God opened your eyes to resources that you had previously overlooked? What "well" might you be overlooking right now?

 GOING DEEPER:
If your group has time and/or wants a challenge, go on to these questions.

---

8. Do God's words in verses 12 and 13 fully excuse Abraham for his actions? What do you think Abraham should have done in this situation?

9. God gave Hagar both help with her immediate problem (the well) and a hope to sustain her into the future (a promise for her son). Which do you most need right now?

 Caring Time : 15 min.
APPLY THE LESSON AND PRAY FOR ONE ANOTHER

Leader

This very important time is to develop and express your concern for each other as group members by praying for one another. In this first session it is also important to discuss the rules that the group will follow.

1. Have your group agree to its group covenant and ground rules (see the introductory material in the front of this book).

2. Thank God now for what he has provided or for the resources he has made known to you.

3. What resource are you nearly out of right now, that this group can help you restore?
   - ○ Hope for my future.
   - ○ Patience with my children.
   - ○ Faith in God's provision.
   - ○ Trust in the people around me.
   - ○ Other _____.

4. Pray specifically for God to lead you to someone to bring next week to fill the empty chair.

P.S. At the closing pass around your books and have everyone sign the Group Directory inside at the beginning of this book.

 # NEXT WEEK

Today we looked at the story of Hagar and what it says to us about God's provision when we have really tough times. In the coming week, ask God to show you what provisions he has made for you in your Christian walk. Next week we will consider the well known and much loved story of Ruth, and what it says to us about developing and valuing a personal support system. We will be reminded that oftentimes the most valuable resource that God gives us is the support of other people.

 # NOTES ON JOHN 21:1–21

Summary: God had promised a son to Sarah and Abraham, and he had told them that from this son a great nation would come (Gen. 12:1–3; 15:1–6; 18:10–15.) When Sarah remained without children into her old age, however, she convinced Abraham to take her Egyptian maid Hagar as his concubine and have a child by her (Gen. 16:1–4.). This was considered acceptable in the society of the time. In addition, the child could be a legal heir and would take some of the onus off of Sarah for not having provided one. The "plot thickens" however when Sarah herself later becomes pregnant (at age 90!) and bears a son. This causes Sarah to change her attitude entirely about Hagar and her son, and she demands that they be exiled. After God promises to care for the boy, Abraham does so. Hagar and her son end up out of food and water in the middle of the desert of Beersheba. Just when she is ready to give up, God provides her with water and a promise of hope for the boy's future.

21:1 did...as he had promised.
This reminds us that God is true to his promises. The arrangement with Hagar was made because they hadn't fully trusted this promise.

21:3 Isaac. The name means "he laughs." Abraham once laughed, scoffing at the idea of fathering a son at his age (17:17). Sarah had laughed, too (18:12). This time the laughter was happier, and was a response to God's faithfulness, instead of being an indication of skepticism of that faithfulness.

21:4 eight days old. God had commanded in Genesis 17:10–12 that every male among them should be circumcised when he is eight days old.

21:5 God promised Abraham, now 100 years old, that he would be the father of a son by Sarah (17:16–17).

21:8 was weaned. It was customary to wean a child around the age of three, and to hold a celebration of this occasion.

21:9 mocking. We cannot know what Ishmael had done that was interpreted by Sarah as mocking, or whether her perception was justified. At the time Ishmael would have been seventeen and Isaac three, a difference which normally doesn't lend itself to sibling rivalry. In an earlier story, Sarah complained that Hagar herself was making fun of her (Gen. 16:4–5).

21:12 it is through Isaac that your offspring will be reckoned. God had promised Abraham offspring as numerous as the stars of heaven (Gen. 15:4–6).

21:13 a nation also. Ishmael was the father of the Ishmaelites (see Gen. 25:12–18; 37:28) who are considered ancestors of the Arab nations.

21:14 Despite certain anxiety, Abraham obeyed God's command immediately, even though it meant being away from Ishmael.

21:17 God heard. The name Ishmael means "God hears."

21:19 God opened her eyes. Hagar's grief was so deep that God had to open her eyes so she could see the much-needed water. The Old Testament often uses a spring or water well to symbolize both spiritual and physical salvation.

21:21 his mother got a wife for him from Egypt. Hagar procured a wife for her son from her own nation.

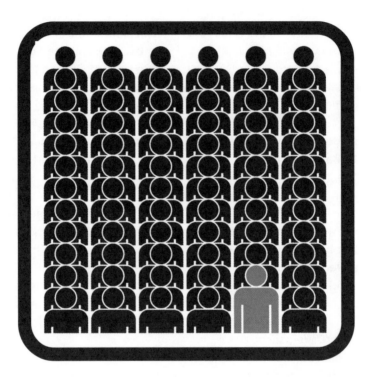

BEING SINGLE AND
THE SPIRITUAL QUEST

Session 2
RUTH: MAINTAINING A SUPPORT SYSTEM

Scripture **Ruth 1:1-18**

LAST WEEK

In last week's session we heard the story of Hagar and we saw how God provided for her by giving her a source of hope and opening her eyes to the resources around her. One of the most important resources we are given by God is other people. For each of us God provides other people who are going through what we are going through, and who can support us. This week we will study about Ruth, a young widow who exemplified this truth. After she lost her husband, she held on tightly to an intimate relationship with her mother-in-law, who was also widowed. Together they found love and support in their hard times.

Icebreaker : 15 min.
CONNECT WITH YOUR GROUP

Leader

Begin this session with a word of prayer. Then, to help your group members get acquainted, introduce each person and take turns answering one or two of the Icebreaker questions. Be sure that everyone gets a chance to participate.

Some of us live in one place most or all of our lives, while others of us move around so much that we lose count of all the places we have been. Which is closest to your own story? Share something about yourself by answering the following "moving" questions.

1. Where do you consider home to be? What is it that you like best about this place?

2. What is the farthest you have been away from home and what caused you to go there?

3. If you could spend a few years living in a country other than the one you are living in now, what country would you want to live in? What appeals to you about that country?

Bible Study : 30 min.
READ SCRIPTURE ÷ DISCUSS

Even though the best known verse from this story (1:16) is often used in weddings, it is at heart the story of the relationship among three single women. The intriguing thing is that they weren't even from the same country. Naomi was from the land of Israel, while Orpah and Ruth were from Moab, an arch-enemy of Israel. Still, Ruth and Naomi especially developed a sense of caring for each other that puts many families to shame. As you read the story, note the things that made this support system so special.

Narrator: In the days when the judges ruled, there was a famine in the land, and a man from Bethlehem in Judah, together with his wife and two sons, went to live for a while in the country of Moab. ²The man's name was Elimelech, his wife's name Naomi, and the names of his two sons were Mahlon and Kilion. They were Ephrathites from Bethlehem, Judah. And they went to Moab and lived there.³Now Elimelech, Naomi's husband, died, and she was left with her two sons. ⁴They married Moabite women, one named Orpah and the other Ruth. After they had lived there about ten years, ⁵both Mahlon and Kilion also died, and Naomi was left without her two sons and her husband. ⁶When she heard in Moab that the Lord had come to the aid of his people by providing food for them, Naomi and her daughters-in-law prepared to return home from there. ⁷With her two daughters-in-law she left the place where she had been living and set out on the road that would take them back to the land of Judah. ⁸Then Naomi said to her two daughters-in-law,

Naomi: "Go back, each of you, to your mother's home. May the Lord show kindness to you, as you have shown to your dead and to me. ⁹May the Lord grant that each of you will find rest in the home of another husband."

Narrator: Then she kissed them and they wept aloud ¹⁰and said to her,

Ruth: "We will go back with you to your people."

Narrator:	[11]But Naomi said
Naomi:	"Return home, my daughters. Why would you come with me? Am I going to have any more sons, who could become your husbands? [12]Return home, my daughters; I am too old to have another husband. Even if I thought there was still hope for me – even if I had a husband tonight and then gave birth to sons [13]would you wait until they grew up? Would you remain unmarried for them? No, my daughters. It is more bitter for me than for you, because the Lord's hand has gone out against me!"
Narrator:	[14]At this they wept again. Then Orpah kissed her mother-in-law good-by, but Ruth clung to her.
Naomi:	[15]"Look," said Naomi, "your sister-in-law is going back to her people and her gods. Go back with her."
Narrator:	[16]But Ruth replied
Ruth:	"Don't urge me to leave you or to turn back from you. Where you go I will go, and where you stay I will stay. Your people will be my people and your God my God. [17]Where you die I will die, and there I will be buried. May the Lord deal with me, be it ever so severely, if anything but death separates you and me."
Narrator:	[18]When Naomi realized that Ruth was determined to go with her, she stopped urging her.

Ruth 1:1–18 (NIV)

 QUESTIONS FOR INTERACTION

Leader

Refer to the Summary and Study Notes at the end of this section as needed. If 30 minutes is not enough time to answer all of the questions in this section, conclude the Bible Study by answering questions 7 and 8.

1. What kind of "famine" have you found yourself going through most often in your life?
   ○ An economic famine: too many bills, too little money.
   ○ A famine in my social life: another Saturday night and I ain't got nobody.

○ A spiritual famine: my soul is dry and parched.
○ An emotional famine: it is all I can do to keep going.
○ A vocational famine: work is meaningless.
○ Other _____.

2. Why does Naomi advise her daughters-in-law to go back home after the men all died?

3. Why does Naomi think that Orpah and Ruth will be better off going back to the homes of their mothers? Does her advice seem good to you?

4. What makes Ruth so determined to stick with Naomi, in spite of Naomi's advice?
○ She didn't want to lose anyone else whom she had become close to.
○ She thought Naomi needed her.
○ Sometimes your closest relationships aren't blood relationships.
○ She was scared of change.
○ She didn't want to be seen as a "fair-weather friend."
○ Other _____.

6. How might it have been helpful for both women to have another single woman to lean on?

7. When did you last have a friend who showed the kind of loyalty to you that Ruth showed to Naomi? What factors build this kind of loyalty? What do you need to do to have more friendships like this one?

8. Ruth learned of God through Naomi. What friendship has most helped you learn about God?

 GOING DEEPER:
If your group has time and/or wants a challenge, go on to these questions.

9. Ruth had to decide between what seemed to be in her own best interests (going to her own home where she would more likely find a husband) and loyalty to Naomi. When should a person show loyalty, and when should a person look after personal interest?

10. What made Naomi feel that "the Lord's hand had gone out against her"? What might you say to someone who felt this way?

Caring Time : 15 min.
APPLY THE LESSON AND PRAY FOR ONE ANOTHER

Leader

Bring the group members back together and begin the Caring Time by sharing responses to all three questions. Then take turns sharing prayer requests and having a time of group prayer.

1. Take time to thank God for the friendships you shared about in questions 7 and 8 above. Ask Him to teach you how to be such a friend to someone else who may be alone.

2. What "famine" are you facing right now that you need this group to pray about? Are there other ways this group can help with this need?

3. Pray specifically for God to lead you to someone to bring next week to fill the empty chair.

NEXT WEEK

Today we considered the story of Ruth, and what it says to us about our own personal support system. We were reminded that oftentimes the most valuable resource that God gives us is the support of other people. In the coming week, take time to give thanks to God—and to special friends—for the support that those friends have given you. Next week we will move to the New Testament and look at a story about two single sisters who lived together: Mary and Martha. We will seek to learn from their contrasting styles what it means to develop spiritual priorities in the midst of the hectic pace of life.

NOTES ON RUTH 1:1–18

Summary: Naomi went through one of those periods in life when one bad thing piles on top of another. She and her family were in Judah at the time of a famine, and in order to provide for the family, they moved to Moab, a foreign country. In

Moab their sons married wives, but not long after they did so, the father died and then the two married sons died, leaving Naomi and two grieving widows as daughters-in-law. When Naomi decided to return to Judah, she tried to convince her daughters-in-law, Orpah and Ruth, to return to their mothers' houses. Orpah eventually took the advice, but Ruth declared her undying loyalty, and hence became an example of faithfulness for all generations

---

1:1 when the judges ruled. These events happened after the Hebrews settled in the Promised Land, but before they received their first king, Saul. The Book of Judges precedes Ruth. This is significant because Judges is full of stories of Israel's unfaithfulness, while Ruth tells the story of a foreigner's faithfulness. Bethlehem. The Bethlehem where Jesus was born. This is significant because Ruth eventually marries Boaz and becomes the great-grandmother of King David and an ancestor of Jesus (see Matt. 1: 5–6, 16).

1:3 Naomi's husband, died. In these times a widow was destitute since women were often unable to work for a living. Naomi was even more at a disadvantage being a widow in a foreign land.

1:4 Moabite. The Moabites were descendants of Lot's son Moab (Gen. 19:36-37). Lot was Abraham's nephew. Whether marriage to such Moabite women was lawful is open to debate. Solomon was chastised for marrying many foreign women, including Moabites (1 Kings 11:1–5), and 1 Kings 11:2 says, "They were from the nations about which the Lord had told the Israelites, 'You must not intermarry with them...'" Also Deuteronomy 23:3 says, "No Ammonite or Moabite or any of his descendants may enter the assembly of the Lord, even down to the tenth generation." This is important since King David was the descendent of Ruth the Moabitess, and he was only the third generation down.

1:5 without her two sons and her husband. Naomi was left alone, but in her culture that wasn't the worst of it. She was left with no one to carry on her family name and bloodline, which was of the utmost importance in that day and time.

1:8 Go back. For several reasons Naomi would have seen the prospects for her daughters-in-law as bleak. Since she was widowed and alone, she could offer them few resources. Also, their prospects for marriage back in Bethlehem would be diminished since they were foreigners. **kindness**. The particular brand of kindness described here speaks of God's grace and his loyalty to his covenant people. These women had been good to Naomi and her family. Now she was blessing them with the gracious kindness of God.

1:10 "We will go back with you to your people." This initial offer would have been considered the polite thing to do. Only persistence would demonstrate a sincere intent to stick with Naomi.

1:11 Am I going to have any more sons...? According to the Law, when a woman was widowed, her deceased husband's closest male relative (often a brother) would step in and care for her. This kept the family inheritance intact. As it stood, Naomi had no one else to offer these women to care for them. **your husbands**. In these ancient days an unmarried woman had no security. Naomi was doing right for Orpah and Ruth to think first and foremost about their marital status.

1:12 I am too old. Naomi seems to feel that her options are completely depleted. In this culture a woman's role was to bear children, particularly sons. At one time Naomi had fulfilled that role, but now it had all been taken from her. A lifetime of effort was gone and she had nothing to show for it. She refers to this emptiness in verse 21.

1:13 more bitter. Naomi later asks to be called "Mara" which means "bitter" (v. 20). the Lord's hand has gone out against me! All personal tragedy was felt at this time to be due to the judgment of God. Job questions this, and Jesus refutes the idea altogether (see Luke 13:1–5; John 9:1–3).

1:14 Ruth clung to her. For all Ruth knew at that moment, she was giving up everything that mattered to a woman at that time in order to be loyal to Naomi. This supreme sacrifice on Ruth's part was rewarded in unexpected ways.

1:15 gods. The chief god of Moab was Chemosh. At this point, it must have seemed to Naomi that there was more hope for her daughters-in-law in a culture of false worship than for three women alone traveling from Moab to Bethlehem.

1:16 Ruth made an amazing commitment and sacrifice. She gave up her national identity, her religion, her home, and her own personal journey with no promise of any recompense except to share in Naomi's sorrow. **your God my God**. Whereas Israel had been warned against marrying foreign women because such women could lure them from the true God, this foreign woman was brought to God through her marriage.

1:17 the Lord. This amounted to a confession of faith for Ruth. She did not swear her loyalty according to her national gods, but by Naomi's God, "Yahweh."

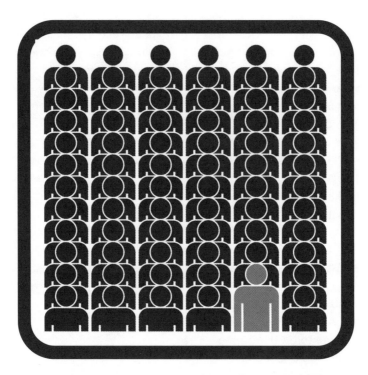

BEING SINGLE AND
THE SPIRITUAL QUEST

Session 3

MARY AND MARTHA: SETTING PRIORITIES

Scripture Luke 10:38–42

 ## LAST WEEK

In our session last week, we talked about Ruth, a young widow who exemplified faithfulness and loyalty, and in so doing demonstrated what makes a great support system for singles. This week we will look at two single sisters, Mary and Martha, who had different priorities in life. Through their example, we will learn how to keep our own priorities straight as we seek to be God's people.

 ### Icebreaker : 15 min.
CONNECT WITH YOUR GROUP

Leader
Choose one or two Icebreaker questions. If you have a new group member you may want to do all three. Remember to stick closely to the three-part agenda and the time allowed for each segment.

In order to function as a family, we all have to perform our various roles. What role have you most frequently performed? Share something about yourself by answering the following questions.

1. In the home in which you lived as a teenager, what person filled each of the following "appliance" roles?
    ○ The vacuum cleaner—the one who kept things tidy.
    ○ The thermostat—the one who kept people comfortable.
    ○ The refrigerator—the one who provided "the goodies."
    ○ The clothes washer—the one who kept things "agitated."
    ○ The window—the one who let the sunshine in.
    ○ The power screwdriver—the one who held things together.
    ○ The television—the one who was the family entertainer.

2. What person in your life right now fills an essential function that you would have a hard time doing yourself?

3. What is one role that you take in relation to your family or friends that you would really like to relinquish to someone else?

Bible Study : 30 min.
READ SCRIPTURE + DISCUSS

Leader

Select a person from your group to read the following story from Luke 10:38–42. Then discuss the Questions for Interaction, dividing into subgroups of three to six. Be sure to save time at the end for the Caring Time.

Mary and Martha were two single women who lived near their brother Lazarus (see John 11:1–44). Even though they were sisters—or perhaps because they were sisters—they had contrasting personalities, and played distinctly different roles in their home.

In the following story, Jesus was not showing a preference for one personality over the other, but rather he was saying something about setting the right priority for the right time. That is an essential skill to develop if we are to make progress in our spiritual lives. As you read the story and answer the questions that follow, consider what it says about your own priorities.

³⁸ While they were traveling, He entered a village, and a woman named Martha welcomed Him into her home. ³⁹ She had a sister named Mary, who also sat at the Lord's feet and was listening to what He said. ⁴⁰ But Martha was distracted by her many tasks, and she came up and asked, "Lord, don't You care that my sister has left me to serve alone? So tell her to give me a hand."

⁴¹ The Lord answered her, "Martha, Martha, you are worried and upset about many things, ⁴² but one thing is necessary. Mary has made the right choice, and it will not be taken away from her."

Luke 10:38–42

QUESTIONS FOR INTERACTION

Leader

Refer to the Summary and Study Notes at the end of this section as needed. If 30 minutes is not enough time to answer all of the questions in this section, conclude the Bible Study by answering questions 6 and 7.

1. Which of the two sisters in this story are you most like at this point in your life?

2. What surprises you most about this story?

○ That in some respects people's behavior hasn't changed much in 2,000 years.
○ That Jesus seemed to side with a "slacker."
○ That someone could really think about cooking and cleaning with Jesus in the house.
○ Other _____.

3. How would you describe Martha's mood as she talks with Jesus about her concern?
○ Panicky.
○ Bossy and controlling.
○ Desperate.
○ Angry.
○ Full of self-pity.
○ Feeling unappreciated.
○ Other _____.

4. What seems to be Martha's highest priority in this story? What priority does Mary seem to have?

5. How might the fact that Martha is single have influenced her responses? What about Mary? How do you see similar responses in your own life as a single person?

6. What are the things you have a tendency to get worried and upset about? Does being single bring anxieties or concerns that married people don't necessarily face? How can Jesus help with these?

7. What priorities would you have to rearrange in order to spend more time at the feet of Jesus?

 GOING DEEPER:
If your group has time and/or wants a challenge, go on to these questions.

---

8. When might Jesus affirm a work-oriented approach like Martha's over the more laid-back approach of Mary? How do Paul's words in 2 Thessalonians 3:6–10 fit in?

9. How do you go about deciding when is the time to focus on the practicalities of getting work done, and when is the time to stop all the hectic activity and be with Jesus?

Caring Time : 15 min.

APPLY THE LESSON AND PRAY FOR ONE ANOTHER

Leader

Begin the Caring Time by having group members take turns sharing responses to all three questions. Be sure to save at least the last five minutes for a time of group prayer. Remember to include a prayer for the empty chair when concluding the prayer time.

1. Which of the worries you spoke of in question 6 above would you most like the group to pray about?

2. How can this group be supportive of you in your efforts to develop a more disciplined devotional life?

3. If you were at the feet of Jesus right now, what question would you like to ask him?

NEXT WEEK

Today we gave some thought to Mary and Martha and what it means to develop spiritual priorities in the midst of the hectic pace of life. In the coming week, deliberately make more time in your schedule to "sit at Jesus' feet." Next week we will take a look at Mary Magdalene and what we can learn from her faithfulness. Because of her servant mindset, she was one of the first to witness the resurrection of Christ. Learning from her can help us also to better serve our Lord.

NOTES ON LUKE 10:38-42

Summary: As Jesus traveled around the countryside away from his home base of Capernaum and Nazareth, he depended on supporters to provide him with a place to stay and food to eat. Mary and Martha, who lived in Bethany, were important supporters of this kind. On this occasion, Martha got overly wrapped up in making provision for the traveling band of disciples, and she got upset at her sister, who chose to spend her time listening to Jesus rather than helping. Jesus, however, told Martha that she should be glad that Mary had her priorities straight—she had chosen to value the spiritual food of Jesus over preoccupation with physical arrangements.

10:38 village. Bethany, just on the outskirts of Jerusalem, was the home of Martha and Mary and their brother Lazarus (whom Jesus raised from the dead). **a woman named Martha**. Martha and Mary also appear in John 11:1–44, where their brother Lazarus dies and is resurrected by Jesus. In that story it is Martha, rather than Mary, who is portrayed as the more faithful one. Martha welcomed Him into her home. It appears that it was Martha's home (she was the head of the household, and probably the older sister), which explains why she would feel more responsibility for the preparations. The family was probably well-off. Lazarus had his own private burial site, and influential people came to the funeral. In addition, on another occasion when this family held a dinner in honor of Jesus, Mary took a pint of expensive perfume and poured it on Jesus' feet (see John 12:1–8.)

10:39 sat at the Lord's feet. Other rabbis did not permit women to sit at their feet while they taught about the Scripture.

10:40 don't you care that my sister has left me to serve alone? This is a classic clash between a disciplined, task-oriented servant (Martha) and a more impulsive, person-oriented student (Mary). Martha says that Mary has left her to do all the work, which assumes the priority that work always comes first over learning and social interaction. Martha emotionalizes the issue by implying that those who don't share her priority don't care. None of this is to say that Jesus sided against the more task-oriented person. He simply says that in this situation, with Jesus himself present for a brief time, stopping to learn from him should be the highest priority, and Mary chose that priority.

10:41 "Martha, Martha, you are worried and upset about many things." Martha is like the thorny soil in which the seed is choked by life's worries (Luke 8:14). Her problem was an inability to focus her life around one central priority. As a result, she tried to be the "superwoman" who "does it all." Jesus calls us to focus our lives around the central priority of the kingdom of God, which then helps all other tasks and goals find their proper place (Matt. 6:25–34).

10:42 but one thing is necessary. Jesus is saying that listening and responding to the Word of the kingdom is the single most important thing in all of life. Mary had chosen to do that, rather than being distracted with the less important expectations of hospitality. Jesus gently commends that attitude to Martha who, in her zeal to serve Jesus, is missing the importance of his presence and his words.

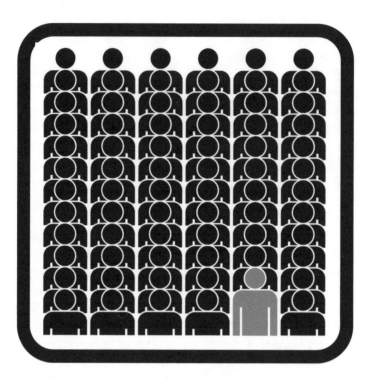

BEING SINGLE AND
THE SPIRITUAL QUEST

Session 4
MARY MAGDALENE: FAITHFUL TO THE END

Scripture John 20:1-18

LAST WEEK

In our session last week, we looked at two single sisters, Mary and Martha, who had different priorities in life. From their priorities we learned something about how to keep our own priorities straight. This week we will consider how Mary Magdalene remained faithful to Jesus even when he was in the grave. We will seek to understand how we can manifest that same kind of faithfulness.

Icebreaker : 15 min.
CONNECT WITH YOUR GROUP

Leader

Choose one, two, or all three of the Icebreaker questions. Welcome and introduce new group members. Be sure that everyone gets a chance to participate.

All of us have had the experience one time or another of misplacing things. Mary Magdalene's "loss" was the result of some good news, but for most of us losing things is highly frustrating. Share your own experience with missing things by answering the following questions.

1. Which of the following do you have the most frustration locating or keeping track of?
   ○ My cell phone.
   ○ My glasses or sunglasses.
   ○ My check book.
   ○ My car in the parking lot.
   ○ My kids.
   ○ Other _____.

2. When you can't find something you need, what is the first thing you generally do?
   ○ Yell and scream.
   ○ Ask whoever else is in the area.
   ○ Retrace my steps.
   ○ Figure it will show up.
   ○ Swear at myself under my breath.
   ○ Other _____.

3. Finish this sentence: "The person I have lost track of who I would really like to re-establish a connection with is...."

 Bible Study : 30 min.
READ SCRIPTURE + DISCUSS

Leader

Select three people from your group to read the following story from John 20:1–18: one should read for Narrator, one for Mary Magdalene, and one for Jesus. Then discuss the Questions for Interaction, dividing into subgroups of three to six. Be sure to save time at the end for the Caring Time.

Mary Magdalene was a single woman out of whom Jesus had cast seven demons. Some traditions said she had once been a prostitute, but we cannot be entirely sure. What we do know is that she showed her appreciation for Jesus by financially supporting his ministry (Luke 8:1–3), and by seeking to care for his body even after his death. Her faithfulness serves as an example to all of us. As you read the story and answer the questions that follow, consider what it says about your own faithfulness or lack of it.

Narrator: On the first day of the week Mary Magdalene came to the tomb early, while it was still dark. She saw that the stone had been removed from the tomb. ² So she ran to Simon Peter and to the other disciple, whom Jesus loved, and said to them,

Mary: "They have taken the Lord out of the tomb, and we don't know where they have put Him!"

Narrator: ³ At that, Peter and the other disciple went out, heading for the tomb. ⁴ The two were running together, but the other disciple outran Peter and got to the tomb first. ⁵ Stooping down, he saw the linen cloths lying there, yet he did not go in. ⁶ Then, following him, Simon Peter came also. He entered the tomb and saw the linen cloths lying there. ⁷ The wrapping that had been on His head was not lying with the linen cloths but folded up in a separate place by itself. ⁸ The other disciple, who had reached the tomb first, then entered the tomb, saw, and believed. ⁹ For they still did not understand the Scripture that He must rise from the dead. ¹⁰ Then the disciples went home again.

Mary: ¹¹ But Mary stood outside facing the tomb, crying. As she was crying, she stooped to look into the tomb. ¹² She saw two angels in white sitting there, one at the head and one at the feet, where Jesus' body had been lying.

Narrator: ¹³ They said to her, "Woman, why are you crying?"

Mary: "Because they've taken away my Lord," she told them, "and I don't know where they've put Him."

Narrator: ¹⁴ Having said this, she turned around and saw Jesus standing there, though she did not know it was Jesus.

Jesus: ¹⁵ "Woman," Jesus said to her, "why are you crying? Who is it you are looking for?"

Narrator: Supposing He was the gardener, she replied,

Mary: "Sir, if you've removed Him, tell me where you've put Him, and I will take Him away."

Jesus: ¹⁶ "Mary!" Jesus said.

Mary: Turning around, she said to Him in Hebrew, "Rabbouni!" —which means "Teacher."

Jesus: ¹⁷ "Don't cling to Me," Jesus told her, "for I have not yet ascended to the Father. But go to My brothers and tell them that I am ascending to My Father and your Father—to My God and your God."

Narrator: ¹⁸ Mary Magdalene went and announced to the disciples,

Mary: "I have seen the Lord!" And she told them what He had said to her

John 20:1–18

QUESTIONS FOR INTERACTION

Leader

Refer to the Summary and Study Notes at the end of this section as needed. If 30 minutes is not enough time to answer all of the questions in this section, conclude the Bible Study by answering questions 6 and 7.

1. Have you ever been called upon to care for a body or take care of "arrangements" after a death? How did you feel about doing so? What part was the most difficult?

2. Mary Magdalene is the only person that all four Gospels say came to the tomb Easter morning. What does it say about her that she came to the tomb to care for the body, while the other disciples did not? Do you think that her singleness might have played a part in this?

3. Suppose that Mary were married. How might her relationship with Jesus have been different then?

4. Why does Jesus not want Mary to hang on to him?
   ○ He didn't like "clingy" people.
   ○ He had work for her to do—spread the good news.
   ○ He didn't want her to get too attached since he would later have to ascend to heaven.
   ○ He had places to go and people to see.
   ○ Other _____.

5. It was doubtless very hard for Mary to get up early and do this task of caring for the body. What similarly difficult task do you feel God is calling you to do right now?

6. If you were married, how might that change your own relationship with Jesus? How might it be deeper? How might it be less intimate?

7. Which of the following acts of Mary Magdalene best describes where you are right now?
   ○ Crying over what is lost.
   ○ Looking all over for Jesus and not knowing when I've found him.
   ○ Hearing Jesus call my name.
   ○ Clinging to Jesus and not wanting to let go.
   ○ Sharing with others what I have seen and experienced.

GOING DEEPER:

If your group has time and/or wants a challenge, go on to these questions.

8. Jesus had predicted his resurrection prior to the crucifixion (see Matt. 16:21; John 16:22–33). Why is it that these predictions don't seem to come to the minds of Mary, Peter, or John (see v. 9) when they find the body gone from the tomb?

9. Mary sees and yet has difficulty believing at first. Thomas insists on seeing before believing (see John 20:24–31). Today, however, we can't see what any of these disciples were privileged to see. What is the relationship between seeing and believing? What is necessary to "open our eyes" to the spiritual realm?

Caring Time : 15 min.
APPLY THE LESSON AND PRAY FOR ONE ANOTHER

Leader

Be sure to save at least 15 minutes for this important time. After sharing responses to all three questions and asking for prayer requests, close in a time of group prayer.

1. What do you feel you need your eyes opened to right now? How can this group help?

2. Mary Magdalene shared her experience with the other disciples. Who do you need to be telling about what Jesus is doing for you?

3. How can this group pray for you in relation to the "difficult task" you shared about in question 5?

NEXT WEEK

Today we gave some thought to Mary Magdalene and what we can learn from her faithful attendance to Jesus after his death. In the coming week, consider what acts of faithfulness might be available to you as a single Christian which might not be so easy for a married person. Next week we will examine Paul's experience as a single male of the time, and we will take a look at what he wrote about the advantages of the single life for a Christian.

 # NOTES ON JOHN 20:1-18

Summary: There couldn't be a more difficult thing a person might have to do than to prepare a loved one's body for burial. In our society, of course, this is most often done by professionals, who are trained for the task, and who generally do not have a personal relationship with the person who died. Mary Magdalene did not have the advantage of this modern convenience. Our text tells us that she went to the tomb on the first day of the week "while it was still dark." That was as early as she could have done it. She could not have done it on the Sabbath, and the Sabbath lasted until sundown Saturday night. So she went at a time when she could do this task with the first rays of the morning's light.

What Mary found totally dumbfounded her. The tomb was empty! For her that could mean but one thing. She had seen him die, so she felt understandably certain that he could not walk away on his own. Someone must have taken the body! The truth dawned on her only slowly. Who could blame her? Resurrection from the dead is not something one normally expects. But it happened, and this is what makes this such a pivotal event in human history. No longer would death have the last word. The door to life beyond death had been opened by Jesus Christ, the Son of God. And that was also the event that turned the discouraged bunch of disciples into a dynamic band that spread throughout the world.

20:1 the first day of the week. This was Sunday. Mary Magdalene. Mary is mentioned in all four Gospel accounts of the Resurrection. Luke 8:2 says that she was one of several women who traveled with the disciples. stone. This account of the burial of Jesus does not mention that the tomb was sealed with a large stone (Matt. 27:60; Mark. 15:46.)

20:2 we don't know where. All other accounts mention that more than one woman came to the tomb that morning, and while John mentions only Mary Magdalene, this "we" may be an acknowledgment that others were involved.

20:5–7 linen cloths...The wrapping. Grave robbers, in search of treasure entombed with the corpse, would either have taken the body still wrapped up, or scattered the linen cloths as they tore them off. The fact that the cloths were neatly laid by was one of the evidences that led the "other disciple" to faith (v. 8).

20:12 two angels in white. The Gospels differ on whether there was one "man" (Mark), or an angel (Matthew), or two "men" (Luke) present. This is not so unusual. In Scripture, angels are often mistaken for men (see Gen. 18:1–15; 19:1–22; Heb. 13:2.)

20:14 she did not know it was Jesus. Whether she was blinded by her intense grief or there was some type of transformation in Jesus' appearance that caused Mary's lack of recognition is not known.

20:15 gardener. The tomb was located in a garden owned by Joseph (Matt. 27:59-6). It would not be unlikely that as an aristocratic member of the Sanhedrin he would employ a gardener to care for his property.

20:16 Mary. When Jesus speaks Mary's name, she immediately recognizes who it is that speaks to her, thus proving her discipleship. **Rabbouni**. Literally, "my teacher." This is not only a title of respect for Jesus, but one that shows Mary's submission and love for him.

20:17 Don't cling to Me. We need not think Jesus refused to allow her to touch him at all, but that, after Mary had expressed the joy and relief she would feel at seeing him, he simply told her that all was not finished yet. She could not hold on to his physical presence because he would soon ascend to the Father.

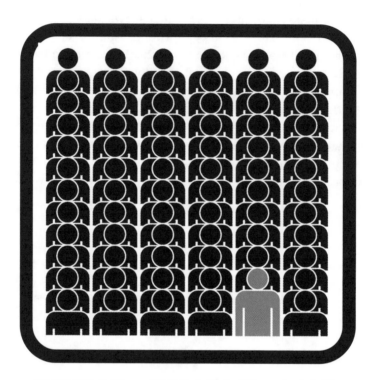

BEING SINGLE AND
THE SPIRITUAL QUEST

Session 5
PAUL: SINGLE-MINDED DEVOTION

Scripture 1 Corinthians 7:1-9, 32-35

LAST WEEK

Last week, we examined the story of Mary Magdalene, and how she remained faithful to Jesus even when he was in the grave. We looked at how we could manifest that same kind of faithfulness. This week we will consider the Apostle Paul, and we will gain an understanding of the advantages of remaining single as a Christian.

Icebreaker : 15 min
CONNECT WITH YOUR GROUP

Leader

Choose one, two, or all three of the Icebreaker questions. Welcome and introduce new group members. Be sure that everyone gets a chance to participate.

In our Scripture for today, Paul writes about wanting Christians "to be free from concern." But the reality is that most of us are not. What has been your history with anxiety? Share your own experience with excess concern by answering the following questions.

1. When you were in school, what was your biggest source of anxiety?
   - ○ Showering in gym class.
   - ○ Talking to the opposite sex.
   - ○ Getting good grades.
   - ○ The changes my body was going through.
   - ○ Making the sports team I wanted to play for.
   - ○ Trying to please my parents.
   - ○ Other _____.

2. When it comes to anxiety as an adult, which of the following are you more like?
   - ○ Alfred E. Newman—"What, me worry?"
   - ○ Charlie Brown—"Good grief!"

3. What are you most likely to be worried or anxious about today?
   ○ World affairs.
   ○ Meeting the right person.
   ○ Money.
   ○ My children.
   ○ My health.
   ○ My career.
   ○ Other _____.

 Bible Study : 30 min.

READ SCRIPTURE ÷ DISCUSS

Leader

Select someone from your group to read the following passage from 1 Corinthians 7:1–9; 32–35. Then discuss the Questions for Interaction, dividing into subgroups of three to six. Be sure to save time at the end for the Caring Time.

Scholars are divided about whether or not Paul was single all of his life. Some think he was, while others believe he was probably a widower (see Notes below). In any case, by the time we hear from him in this passage from 1 Corinthians, he was most certainly single. Unlike some of us, however, he did not view being single as a bad thing. When it came to living his life for Christ, he saw it as a definite advantage. His "single minded" devotion can serve as a model for us. As you read the passage and answer the questions that follow, consider how your own singleness is both an advantage and a disadvantage in your Christian walk.

7About the things you wrote: "It is good for a man not to have relations with a woman." ² But because of sexual immorality, each man should have his own wife, and each woman should have her own husband. ³ A husband should fulfill his marital duty to his wife, and likewise a wife to her husband. ⁴ A wife does not have authority over her own body, but her husband does. Equally, a husband does not have authority over his own body, but his wife does. ⁵ Do not deprive one another— except when you agree, for a time, to devote yourselves to prayer. Then come together again; otherwise, Satan may tempt you because of your lack of self-control. ⁶ I say this as a concession, not as a command. ⁷ I wish that all people were just like me. But each has his own gift from God, one this and another that.

⁸ I say to the unmarried and to widows: It is good for them if they remain as I am. ⁹ But if they do not have self-control, they should marry, for it is better to marry than to burn with desire.

³² I want you to be without concerns. An unmarried man is concerned about the

things of the Lord—how he may please the Lord. [33] But a married man is concerned about the things of the world—how he may please his wife— [34] and he is divided. An unmarried woman or a virgin is concerned about the things of the Lord, so that she may be holy both in body and in spirit. But a married woman is concerned about the things of the world—how she may please her husband. [35] Now I am saying this for your own benefit, not to put a restraint on you, but because of what is proper, and so that you may be devoted to the Lord without distraction.

1 Corinthians 7:1–9, 32–35

 # QUESTIONS FOR INTERACTION

Leader

Refer to the Summary and Study Notes at the end of this section as needed. If 30 minutes is not enough time to answer all of the questions in this section, conclude the Bible Study by answering questions 6 and 7.

1. What surprises you the most about what Paul says here?
   - ○ That Paul would say a husband's body belongs to his wife and vice versa.
   - ○ That Paul does not seem to be anti-sex.
   - ○ That anyone would actually think there are advantages to being single.
   - ○ Other _____.

2. In the society of Paul's time, verse 4 was unusual for its egalitarian emphasis. Do people today believe what Paul says here, or is such equality only theoretical? Have the scales swung in the opposite direction today from Paul's day?

3. Paul describes his ability to be single and celibate as a "gift." What helps a single to have this kind of sexual discipline? What makes it more difficult to have such discipline?

4. What does Paul say in verses 32–34 about the advantages of being single? Is his argument convincing to you, or is this just a "sour grapes" argument?

5. What does Paul say in verse 35 about the way we should live? Is this an appropriate goal for Christians today?

6. What "distractions" do you find compromising your own devotion to the Lord? What can you be doing to reduce or eliminate such distractions?

7. What opportunities for serving God might be more available to you since you are single? What should you be doing right now to act on those opportunities?

GOING DEEPER:

If your group has time and/or wants a challenge, go on to these questions.

8. Is lack of sexual self-control a good reason for marrying, as Paul suggests? Why or why not?

9. Does being "devoted to the Lord without distraction" mean that we should not expect to have a life outside of the church? How should other life interests and involvement relate to what we do for the Lord?

Caring Time : 15 min.

APPLY THE LESSON AND PRAY FOR ONE ANOTHER

Leader

Be sure to save at least 15 minutes for this time of prayer and encouragement. Continue to encourage group members to invite new people to the group.

1. What did the person on your right share about the "distractions" in his or her life? Take time to pray for that person in relation to these "distractions."

2. How can this group pray for you in relation to the opportunities for service you talked about in question 7?

3. Take time to pray for the "empty chair." What single person do you know who might fill that chair next week?

NEXT WEEK

Today we examined Paul's experience as a single male of the time, and we took a look at what he wrote about the advantages of the single life for a Christian. In the coming week, seek ways in which you can find real fulfillment in serving the Lord, doing things that you might not be able to do when married. Next week we will consider the story of Lydia, a wealthy single business woman who after her conversion opened her home to host Paul's missionary work. We will seek to learn from her example about what it means to open not only our homes but our hearts to the people and work of God.

NOTES ON 1 CORINTHIANS 7:1-9, 32-35

Summary: When Paul wrote letters, he wrote not just to tell the recipients what he wanted them to know all along, but to respond to specific questions they had posed to him in their letters. Such was the case in this passage. Specifically, he was responding to some in the Corinthian church who asked whether Christians should be having sex at all, even in marriage. Paul, believing that Christ would be returning soon, said that it would be best for all Christians to be single and celibate. However, because some would not be able to have the self-discipline to handle that, they should go ahead and marry.

A central reason why Paul felt that it was best to be single was that the single person could put more time and energy into serving Christ. Married people owed each other a certain amount of their time and devotion, a commitment that single people do not have.

7:1 you wrote. Up to this point Paul has been dealing with matters reported to him, but now he responds to a series of concerns about which the Corinthian Christians have written. **to have relations with**. The phrase is literally, "to touch a woman," and is a common euphemism for sexual intercourse. This is quite possibly a slogan that reflects the position of an ascetic group within the Corinthian church which felt that Christian husbands who wanted to be spiritual ought to refrain from sexual intercourse with their wives. Or, Paul may have been responding to a question from the Corinthians along the lines of "Is it bad for a man not to marry?"

7:2 First, Paul says that it is not good for a husband and a wife to abstain from sexual relationship, since this will increase the temptation to commit adultery.

7:3–4 Paul now gives the reasons for his views: There is to be complete mutuality within marriage in the matter of sexual rights. This statement stands in sharp contrast to the consensus of the first century, which held that it was the husband alone who had sexual rights and the wife simply submitted to him. For Paul, marriage is a partnership.

7:5 Abstinence is allowed under two conditions: both partners agree, and it is for a limited time. deprive. Literally, "rob." For one partner to opt out of sexual relations under the guise of spirituality is a form of robbery. **prayer**. The purpose of such abstinence is prayer. lack of self-control. Paul assumes that a couple would not be married in the first place if they did not feel any sexual desire, and thus they ought to fulfill such desires legitimately, lest they be tempted to adultery.

7:7 were just like me. That is, celibate. **gift**. Paul states that celibacy is a spiritual gift. It is not a gift that everyone has.

7:8 to the unmarried and to widows. The word translated "unmarried" probably refers here to widowers, so that these words are directed to those who are now unmarried due to the loss of a spouse. **remain as I am**. While Paul may always have been a bachelor, it is more likely that he was a widower, since it was quite rare for a rabbi to be unmarried. In fact, marriage was virtually obligatory for a Jewish man. If a man did not marry and have children, he was said to have "slain his posterity."

7:9 do not have self-control. Abstinence would be a particular problem for those who had once experienced an active married life. **to burn with desire**. When one is consumed with desire, that preoccupation makes it difficult to lead a devoted Christian life.

7:32–35 Paul offers his second reason for preferring singleness: it enables a person to devote more energy to the service of the Lord.

7:34 he is divided. The married man is rightly concerned about how to please the Lord, and equally right in his concern to please his wife. This is the problem: how to be fully faithful to both legitimate commitments. **a married woman**. The same is true of a married woman: her attention is divided in a way not true of a single woman.

7:35 not to put a restraint on you. Literally, "not to put a halter around your neck," as one would do in order to domesticate an animal.

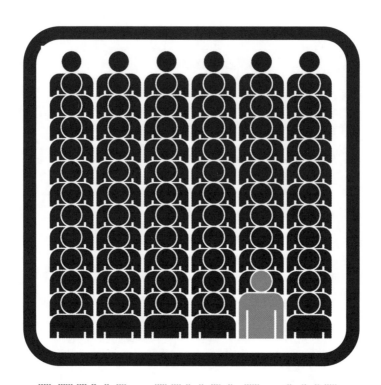

BEING SINGLE AND
THE SPIRITUAL QUEST

Session 6
LYDIA: OPEN HOUSE, OPEN HEART

Scripture **Acts 16:11-15, 35-40**

LAST WEEK

Last week we examined some of what Paul wrote, and we discussed the advantages he believed there were to remaining single as a Christian. This week we will look at Lydia, a wealthy woman who was the first convert in Europe. After her conversion she opened her home to Paul and his missionary work. We will learn from her example about what it means to open not only our homes but our hearts to the people and work of God

Icebreaker : 15 min.
CONNECT WITH YOUR GROUP

Leader

Choose one, two, or all three of the Icebreaker questions. Welcome and introduce new group members. Be sure that everyone gets a chance to participate.

When this group gets together, someone hosts us in their home. But how do you feel about hosting guests in general? Share your own "hospitality history" by answering the following questions.

1. When you were in grade school, who was the most frequent guest you had over to your home?
   ○ Another child from the neighborhood.
   ○ Some adult friends of my parents.
   ○ Some of our extended family.
   ○ Transients needing a place to stay.
   ○ Friends from another town where we used to live.
   ○ We never had guests.
   ○ Other _____.

2. When you know you are going to have guests, what is your first thought?
   - ○ Where can I hide until they leave?
   - ○ Does this mean I can't watch my favorite television shows?
   - ○ Oh, good—someone to talk to!
   - ○ But the house is a mess! Perhaps if I clean all morning....
   - ○ Get out the games!
   - ○ Other _____.

3. If you could invite anyone in the world to your home for one night, whom would you invite and why? What would you plan for the evening?

Bible Study : 30 min.
READ SCRIPTURE + DISCUSS

Leader
Select five people from your group to read the following parts from Acts 16:11–15, 35–40: one person to read for Luke's narration, one person for Lydia, one for the police, one for the jailer, and one for Paul. Then discuss the Questions for Interaction, dividing into subgroups of three to six. Be sure to save time at the end for the Caring Time.

Traveling teachers, such as Jesus and Paul, were generally dependent on their students for room and board as they traveled. Remember, there was no Holiday Inn, Motel 6, or Super 8! In the culture of the time, hospitality was an extremely important and honored virtue. The author of Hebrews declared, "Don't neglect to show hospitality, for by doing this some have welcomed angels as guests without knowing it." (Heb. 13:2). In the following story we learn of one of the people who provided this hospitality for Paul—Lydia of Thyatira. She was evidently a single business woman who dealt in expensive cloth. Once converted, she seemed to know instinctively what role God was calling her to play. She opened her home to Paul and his companions to enable them to better evangelize Philippi and eventually much of Greece. As you read this story and answer the questions that follow, give some thought to how God might be calling you to similar action.

Luke: ¹¹Then, setting sail from Troas, we ran a straight course to Samothrace, the next day to Neapolis, ¹² and from there to Philippi, a Roman colony, which is a leading city of that district of Macedonia. We stayed in that city for a number of days. ¹³ On the Sabbath day we went outside the city gate by the river, where we thought there was a place of prayer. We sat down and spoke to the women gathered there. ¹⁴ A woman named Lydia, a dealer in purple cloth from the city of Thyatira, who worshiped God, was listening. The Lord opened her heart to pay attention to what was spoken by Paul. [15] After she and her household were baptized, she urged us,

Lydia: "If you consider me a believer in the Lord, come and stay at my house."

Luke: And she persuaded us.

Police: [35] When daylight came, the chief magistrates sent the police to say, "Release those men!"

Luke: [36] The jailer reported these words to Paul:

Jailer: "The magistrates have sent orders for you to be released. So come out now and go in peace."

Paul: [37] But Paul said to them, "They beat us in public without a trial, although we are Roman citizens, and threw us in jail. And now are they going to smuggle us out secretly? Certainly not! On the contrary, let them come themselves and escort us out!"

Police: [38] Then the police reported these words to the magistrates.

Luke: And they were afraid when they heard that Paul and Silas were Roman citizens. [39] So they came and apologized to them, and escorting them out, they urged them to leave town. [40] After leaving the jail, they came to Lydia's house where they saw and encouraged the brothers, and departed.

Acts 16:11–15, 35–40

QUESTIONS FOR INTERACTION

Leader

Refer to the Summary and Study Notes at the end of this section as needed. If 30 minutes is not enough time to answer all of the questions in this section, conclude the Bible Study by answering questions 6 and 7.

1. Lydia gathered with her friends outside the city gate at the river. Where is your favorite place to gather with your friends? What are your favorite things to talk about when you gather?

2. What do you think was Lydia's primary motivation for inviting Paul and the others to her home?
   ○ To show it off—she was rich.
   ○ To share her abundance.
   ○ To help with Paul's work.
   ○ To have the opportunity to learn more.
   ○ Other _____.

3. How might Lydia's ministry have been different if she were married? Do you think she'd have provided the same help in that case?

4. Note that "the Lord opened [Lydia's] heart to pay attention to what was spoken by Paul" (v. 14). What do you think this means? How might her singleness have influenced her reaction here?

5. Lydia's first act upon conversion is to be baptized along with "her household" (v. 15). Since she is single, what is meant by her household? How might you, as a single person, have great influence over the spiritual decisions of others?

6. Before Lydia opened her home to Paul, she first opened her heart to Jesus Christ. Where are you in that process?
   ○ Still hanging around the river, looking for inspiration.
   ○ Feeling God's tug on my heart.
   ○ Freshly baptized, looking for my role to play.
   ○ Working hard to encourage others along the same path.

7. Lydia offered her home for the Lord's work. What do you have that the Lord could use in his work right now? What keeps you from offering it?

 GOING DEEPER:
If your group has time and/or wants a challenge, go on to these questions.

---

8. What does it say to you that this church grew and became strong in spite of the fact that Paul had only preached a short time here? How might Lydia (and other single people) have played an important role in that growth?

Caring Time : 15 min.
APPLY THE LESSON AND PRAY FOR ONE ANOTHER

Leader

Following the Caring Time, discuss with your group how they would like to celebrate the last session next week. Also discuss the possibility of continuing with another study.

1. In what area of your life do you most need encouragement this week? How can this group help?

2. What support do you need from this group in relation to what you want to offer to the Lord (question 7)? What do you see as your first step in that direction?

3. Take time to pray for the "empty chair." What single person do you know who might fill that chair next week?

NEXT WEEK

Today we considered the story of Lydia, a wealthy single business woman who opened her home to host Paul's missionary work, and what we can learn from her example. In the coming week, consider opening your own home or some of your personal time and talents to help others as Lydia did. Next week we will look at Jesus himself, and how, though single, he established a family of faith.

NOTES ON ACTS 16:11-15, 35-40

Summary: Sometimes when we talk about the work of Paul, we assume that he did it all by himself—perhaps with a little help from Barnabas and Silas. But the reality is that there were many people who were part of Paul's team and who helped him along the way. Lydia was part of this team for the work Paul did in establishing the gospel in Europe. She opened her home to Paul and Silas and that home became the base for a continuing church in which she probably played a key role. As in most places, of course, Paul's work also met opposition. In Philippi, the first European city in which Paul preached the Gospel, Paul and Silas had to spend some time in prison. This was because Paul healed a slave woman of a spirit that somehow gave her the ability to prophesy. Those who owned her were angry because they had lost their "cash cow." Paul and Silas were even illegally beaten. When they found out that Paul was a Roman citizen and that they had made a big mistake, they tried to just release him quietly, but he would have none of it. He insisted on an official escort out of the prison! Before leaving the city, however, Paul made a point of stopping again at Lydia's home to encourage the believers who now gathered there.

16:14 a dealer in purple cloth. The city of Thyatira was famous for its trade in purple dyes. These dyes were made by taking the glands of the myrax, a purple sea snail, and simmering them in pans for a few days. They then dipped cloth in it for a dye that would never fade. This purple was considered a kingly color, and there were laws in Rome that limited who could wear it. Selling such a luxurious cloth probably meant that Lydia was a wealthy woman.

16:15 she and her household were baptized. Lydia was the first Christian convert in Europe. This was vital since it is from Europe that Christianity spread to the rest of the world. Paul had been led there by a vision of a man from Macedonia. She was probably not married (perhaps widowed) since the text refers to "her household." Had a husband been around it would have been referred to as "his household."

16:35–40 The magistrates simply wanted to expel Paul and Silas from town to avoid any further trouble. However, they refused to go without a personal apology from the magistrates for their breach of justice. This was not simply a matter of self-vindication nor a matter of insisting on the proper administration of justice—as deserved as these things were under the circum-

stances. It was especially important for the protection of the young church in Philippi since Paul's claim to citizenship showed that he was not interested in violating Roman customs as he had been charged (v.21). By being escorted out of the prison by the magistrates, a signal would be communicated to the community at large that the charges had been false. As a result, the community would be more likely to leave the young church alone.

16:37 While local magistrates could execute punishment upon troublemakers without a trial, that was never to be the case when it was a Roman citizen who was charged. Citizenship included the right to a trial for any accusations. In the Roman empire, most residents did not have the legal protection or status of a citizen. Citizenship was conferred only upon those born in certain cities (as in Paul's case), or those who could afford to pay for the privilege (22:28). The magistrates had overlooked the possibility that these two Jews might be citizens. If Paul reported their action to a higher authority, they could be in danger of losing their office.

16:39-40 The magistrates did what they could to appease Paul and Silas, but still asked them to leave the city to avoid any further commotion in the community. Had that occurred, Paul and Silas would have had to be imprisoned for their safety until trial. Not wanting to face the possibility of that type of detention, the missionaries encouraged the young church and went on to Thessalonica. Since the next "we" section does not occur until Paul passes through Macedonia once again (20:5), Luke apparently was left behind to strengthen the young church and train its leaders.

Lydia's house. Lydia's house now seems to be the location of a "house church" where believers met to worship and find encouragement. Meeting in church buildings designed for that purpose did not happen until much later. Chloe was probably another woman whose home was used in this way as a house church (see 1 Cor. 1:11.)

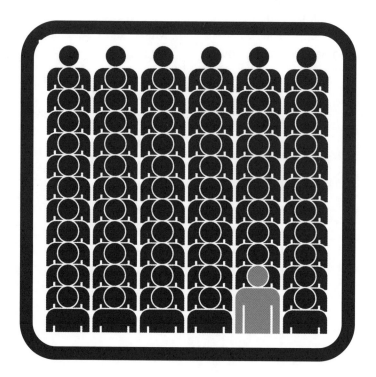

BEING SINGLE AND
THE SPIRITUAL QUEST

Session 7
JESUS: A FAMILY OF FAITH

Scripture Mark 3:13-35

 ## LAST WEEK

Last week we looked at Lydia, and how she opened her home to Paul and his missionary work. This week we will seek a deeper understanding of how Jesus lived as a single adult, and how he developed a family, not among those who were related by blood but among those bound together by caring and obedience to God. We will consider how we too can be part of such a family of faith.

 ## Icebreaker : 15 min.
CONNECT WITH YOUR GROUP

Leader
Answer both Icebreaker questions, and be sure that everyone gets a chance to participate.

Several of those Jesus appointed as apostles had nicknames. Such names can convey more about a person than their original given name. Explore nicknames and learn more about each other by answering the following questions.

1. What nickname did you have when you were growing up? Where did you get this nickname and how did you feel about it?

2. Over the course of this study we have gotten to know each other much better. What can you affirm in your fellow group members by giving them one of the following biblical nicknames? (This works best if you disregard whether they are male or female names!)
   - "Peter"—meaning "rock," the one who was solid and dependable(3:16).
   - "Boanerges"—meaning "Sons of Thunder," the one who spoke with power(3:17).
   - "Barnabas"—meaning "son of encouragement" (Acts 4:36), the one who knew what to say to lift others up.
   - "Didymus"—meaning "Twin" (John 11:16), the one in the group who was most like me.
   - "Naomi"—meaning "pleasantness" (Ruth 1:20), the one who always seemed easy to get along with.
   - "Isaac"—meaning "he laughs" (Gen. 17:19), the one who helped us all to laugh.

○ "Eve"—meaning "living" (Gen.3:20), the one who brought life to the group.

○ "Moses" – meaning "to draw out" (Ex. 2:10), the one who drew others out and got us talking.

○ "Esther"—meaning "star" (Esther 2:7), the one who shone brightly and led us to the hope.

Bible Study : 30 min.
READ SCRIPTURE ÷ DISCUSS

Leader

Select two people from your group to read the following parts from Mark 3:13–35: one for the narrator, and the other for Jesus. Then discuss the Questions for Interaction, dividing into subgroups of three to six. Be sure to save time at the end for the Caring Time.

Jesus never married, but he had a family. His family, according to his words, did the will of his Father who was in heaven. His disciples, the principle ones of which are named in this passage, were his family. The members of the biological family into which he was born seemed to have taken a while to truly understand him and his role, and he had to rebuke them for this. Eventually they seemed to understand, and became part of his spiritual family as well. As you read the following, think of what it says to you about what "family" is:

Narrator: ¹³ Then He went up the mountain and summoned those He wanted, and they came to Him. ¹⁴ He appointed 12, whom He also named apostles, that they might be with Him and that He might send them out to preach ¹⁵ and to have authority to drive out demons. ¹⁶ He appointed the Twelve: To Simon, He gave the name Peter; ¹⁷ and to James the son of Zebedee, and to his brother John, He gave the name "Boanerges" (that is, "Sons of Thunder"); ¹⁸ Andrew; Philip and Bartholomew; Matthew and Thomas; James the son of Alphaeus, and Thaddaeus; Simon the Zealot, ¹⁹ and Judas Iscariot, who also betrayed Him. ²⁰ Then He went into a house, and the crowd gathered again so that they were not even able to eat. ²¹ When His family heard this, they set out to restrain Him, because they said, "He's out of His mind." ²² And the scribes who had come down from Jerusalem said, "He has Beelzebul in Him!" and, "He drives out demons by the ruler of the demons!"

Jesus: 23 So He summoned them and spoke to them in parables: "How can Satan drive out Satan? 24 If a kingdom is divided against itself, that kingdom cannot stand. 25 If a house is divided against itself, that house cannot stand. 26 And if Satan rebels against himself and is divided, he cannot stand but is finished! 27 "On the other hand, no one can enter a strong man's house and rob his possessions unless he first ties up the strong man. Then he will rob his house. 28 I assure you: People will be forgiven for all sins and whatever blasphemies they may blaspheme. 29 But whoever blasphemes against the Holy Spirit never has forgiveness, but is guilty of an eternal sin" —

Narrator: 30 because they were saying, "He has an unclean spirit." 31 Then His mother and His brothers came, and standing outside, they sent word to Him and called Him. 32 A crowd was sitting around Him and told Him, "Look, Your mother, Your brothers, and Your sisters are outside asking for You."

Jesus: 33 He replied to them, "Who are My mother and My brothers?" 34And looking about at those who were sitting in a circle around Him, He said, "Here are My mother and My brothers! 35 Whoever does the will of God is My brother and sister and mother."

Mark 3:13–35

 # QUESTIONS FOR INTERACTION

Leader

Refer to the Summary and Study Notes at the end of this section as needed. If 30 minutes is not enough time to answer all of the questions in this section, conclude the Bible Study by answering questions 6 and 7.

1. In what way do you most identify with Jesus in this story?
   - ○ I also had one I thought was a friend, who betrayed me (v.19).
   - ○ Life also gets hectic for me, so that stopping to eat can even be hard (v.20).
   - ○ My family has also sometimes thought I was crazy (v.21).
   - ○ People have sometimes accused me of some pretty bad things (vv. 22–30).
   - ○ I also have found a group of people who were more like family than my biological family (vv. 31–35).
   - ○ Other _____.

2. The 12 men that Jesus selected were from all walks of life: fishermen, tax collectors, radicals, conservatives. What are the requirements for being a disciple of Jesus today? How can a single person fulfill the role as a disciple different than a married person can?

3. Why do you think that Jesus' family thought he was out of his mind?
   ○ They thought such a hectic life would drive anyone crazy.
   ○ They were hearing claims about him that they couldn't believe (see 3:11).
   ○ They figured that challenging tradition and powerful leaders was crazy (see 2:23– 3:6).
   ○ It was just a matter of a mother who felt she was losing control of her son.
   ○ Other _____.

4. What are the implications of Jesus' teaching (v. 33–35) for single people? For married people?

5. Have you ever experienced conflict between what God wanted for you and what your family expected of you? Have you ever felt as though you didn't really have a family of your own?

6. What can a single person today do to develop a spiritual family? Where are you in that process?

7. Has this group been a sort of spiritual family for you during this study? How can that continue into the future? How can it improve?

 GOING DEEPER:
If your group has time and/or wants a challenge, go on to these questions.

8. How is what Jesus teaches here different than what cultists do when they try to get converts to separate from their families? To what degree is separating from family healthy, and when is it a danger?

9. If being part of Jesus' family necessitates doing God's will, does that mean we are no longer part of the family if we morally falter? Why or why not? What role do grace and forgiveness play here?

Caring Time : 15 min.
APPLY THE LESSON AND PRAY FOR ONE ANOTHER

Leader

Conclude this final Caring Time by praying for each group member and asking for God's blessing in any plans to start a new group and/or continue to study together.

1. Take time to thank God for each other and for what the group has meant to you.

2. What continuing support do you need in order to remain obedient to God's will as part of Jesus' family?

3. How would you like the group to continue to pray for you?

NOTES ON MARK 3:13–35

Summary: In 1:16–45 Mark described the enthusiasm with which the crowds greeted Jesus. In 2:1–3:6 he described, in contrast, the hostility the religious leaders had toward Jesus. In this passage he further differentiates the reactions to Jesus. Two groups are for him: the crowds (vv. 7–12) and the disciples (vv. 13–19). Two groups are against him: his family (vv. 20–21, 31–35) and the teachers of the Law (vv. 22–30). His family did eventually come around, as his mother was among those who gathered with the disciples and prayed after the Ascension (Acts 1:14), and James, his brother, became a leader in the early church (see Gal. 1:19 and the letter of James), and another brother, Jude, also seems to have become a believer (the letter of Jude.)

3:16–19 Peter's name heads each list of the apostles; Judas is always last. There are two (possibly three) sets of brothers and several sets of friends. Some of these men are strong-willed and impetuous (e.g., the Sons of Thunder, who want to consume a village with fire in Luke 9:51–56); some are known only from the lists (e.g. Thaddaeus). There are two natural enemies: the pro–government tax collector Matthew (Levi) and the anti–government guerrilla Simon the Zealot.

3:20–21,31–35 For the first time, Jesus' family is heard from, though in a surprising role. They seem to want to stop Jesus' ministry, whether out of good motives (they are concerned that he is not able to take care of himself with the crowds constantly pressing him, v. 20) or out of misunderstanding (he is acting strangely, v. 21).

3:21 set out to restrain Him. Take him home by force (see 6:17, where the same word is translated "arrested"). **out of His mind**. Literally, "he is beside himself." His family concludes that he is suffering from some sort of ecstatic, religiously induced mental illness.

3:22 had come down from Jerusalem. To go from Jerusalem in the south to Galilee in the north, one descends, because Jerusalem stands at an elevation of 2,400 feet above sea level, while the Sea of Galilee was 600 feet below sea level. **He has Beelzebul in Him**. Beelzebul is probably a slang expression for a demon-prince, meaning something like "The Lord of Dung." To be possessed by this demon is to be controlled and empowered by him, which is how the teachers of the Law explained Jesus' miracles. They cannot deny his healing and exorcism, and since they know they are God's representatives (and Jesus is not one of them), the only other source of such power is Satan. The charge that Jesus is a sorcerer was found frequently in Jewish literature until the modern age.

3:23–27 Jesus begins by pointing out the flaw in their argument: the power of Satan cannot be used to undo the power of Satan. Then by means of three brief parables he drives home his point. A kingdom (or even a house) that wars against itself will fall. Furthermore, he has used his power to bind Satan ("the strong man"), as demonstrated by the fact that he is undoing Satan's works every time he heals or casts out a demon.

3:28–29 Jesus ends by stating that all manner of sin will be forgiven ("all the sins and blasphemies of men"). However, in order for forgiveness to be given it must be requested. And the teachers of the Law are so blind that they do not notice the blasphemy in their calling Jesus—who is God's Son—a tool of Satan, the prince of demons. Thus it would never occur to them to ask for forgiveness. To blaspheme against the Holy Spirit is to resist the Spirit's convicting work and thus not to see the sin, and so fail to ask for forgiveness. Anxiety about whether one has committed "an eternal sin" is the very demonstration that one is still open to the convicting work of the Spirit. Jesus warns his critics not to be guilty of the very thing they accused him of in the story of the paralytic (2:7).

3:30 The way the Greek is phrased here indicates that the teachers of the Law had a callous and fixed attitude of mind.

3:31–32 The family's assessment that Jesus is "out of his mind" is a milder version of the claim by the teachers of the Law that "he is possessed by Beelzebub." At this point the family arrives to "take charge" of

Jesus (this is not a friendly visit). They find him surrounded by the crowd (v. 32). Not wanting to confront him in that setting, they send someone to call him out.

3:34–35 Jesus gives a new definition of family. Kinship is not a matter of heredity, it is a matter of spirit; i.e., doing God's will—which his natural family is not doing by trying to stop his ministry. Eventually his family will move from doubt to faith (see John 19:25–27; Acts 1:14; 1 Cor. 15:7).

PERSONAL NOTES

PERSONAL NOTES

PERSONAL NOTES

PERSONAL NOTES

PERSONAL NOTES